Come to the River

Christy Sawyer

www.christysawyerministries.com

COME TO THE RIVER

Foreword

For every woman whose heart cry is more, this book is for you. Christy has a passion to see women walk in victory, and she masterfully gives us insights through her life experiences, pointing the reader to the true POWER, the infilling POWER of the Holy Spirit.

The Bible talks about different types of power, as this Christian walk is supposed to be supernatural in every way. We read in Romans 8:11, "But if the Spirit of Him who raised Jesus from the dead dwells in you..."

Christy understands and exhorts believers to walk in the power, the authority, and the anointing that has been given to the church by Christ. Her message is to inspire believers to desire to live in that power.

Come to the River is filled with rich teaching by Christy and powerful testimonies. If you are looking for a book that will encourage, challenge, and motivate you to grow deeper in your spiritual walk, you found it.

Gail Ross,
Host and Producer of Faith Talk, Christian Radio
Author and Speaker

In the Beginning

On the last and greatest day of the festival, Jesus stood and said in a loud voice, "Let anyone who is thirsty come to me and drink. Whoever believes in Me, as Scripture has said, rivers of living water will flow from within them. By this he meant the Spirit." John 7:37-39

God commands us to be filled with the Spirit, and if we are not filled, it is because we are living beneath our privileges. — D.L. Moody

Sitting on my lanai one fall morning, I was studying and doing my daily devotions. Thoughts of the next series I planned to teach would randomly come in and out of my head. My plan was to begin teaching from the book of Revelation at the first of the year—not an easy subject, I know, but so fascinating that I was ready to dig in.

At that moment, a little check in my spirit messed up my plan, and afterward, I couldn't focus on anything else that morning. I had to close my Bible, my journal, and my books and move to another spot outside and say, "Ok, Lord, I'm listening."

I believe He brought to my mind many of the women I mentor and counsel. I had been experiencing frustration because so many of these women, godly women, could not seem to get victory in their lives. They seemed to be traveling the same wilderness circle over and over again. Although I had certainly prayed with them and for them in the past, that morning I began to have some real talk with God about it.

1

Why? Why won't their situations shift? Why are your women (and men) living defeated lives? How can they represent You to this world if they are poor in spirit themselves? If I'm to be completely transparent, I was asking for myself as well. Where was the power in my own life that I needed so desperately in order to fulfill the calling that God had placed on me?

I believe God spoke to me, though not audibly, that morning and said, "My people are living beneath their privileges. They are settling for a fountain when I have rivers for them." I believe that what He showed me is missing in His people is the power of the Holy Spirit. As happens with me and my Father so often, He got me to the place He wanted me, and then I knew: He wanted me to teach on the Holy Spirit. That sounds easier than Revelation, doesn't it?

When I finally got it, I began to tremble. The Holy Spirit: How vast! How huge! How could I even begin to teach on the subject? Where would I even start? As I imagine He does often, I imagined God rolling His eyes at me and saying, "You will do it with the power of the Holy Spirit, dummy! That's the point!" And so began preparation, with much prayer, for *Unleashed: A Study of the Holy Spirit*. Somehow, I knew in my spirit that this was much bigger than me. I sensed that God was up to something really incredible.

One Sunday morning, a pastor on staff at our church left an urgent message for me on my desk and said she *must* pray for me before the day ended. I went to her at the altar at the close of service that day. She said that the Holy Spirit had placed in her an urgency to pray for me and for my ministry. The word He had given her was "groundswell," which means upsurge, increase, wave, escalation, and outbreak. The series that was to last six to eight weeks lasted eleven months.

I could write an entire book on what happened in that class and how it spilled over into other ministries and into the worship at our church. However, for the purposes of this book, I wanted to share with you the process of how *Come to the River* was birthed. During those eleven months and for months after, something fascinating began to happen in God's women. It was as if they became hungry, and they couldn't get that hunger satisfied.

Some of them came to me and asked me to lead a women's retreat where they could get away and just tarry with the Holy Spirit. An expectation had been building that God would surely do great things. With fear, trembling, and much prayer, it was scheduled. I knew the theme had to be about rivers, and so *Come to the River* was born. I had a number in mind of how many women I expected to come, and that number tripled by the time we got there.

Included in this book are some testimonies of a few of the women who attended, as well as the word the Holy Spirit gave me for the weekend. I pray that you will be blessed and overtaken by the river of God's Spirit as you read.

Rivers

But whoever drinks of the water that I shall give him will never thirst. But the water that I shall give him will become in him a fountain of water springing up into everlasting life. (John 14:14)

"I'll give him a fountain..." Praise God for salvation. Praise Him for the water that Jesus gives that satisfies us. This water causes us to know who we are and who our Redeemer is. He said, "When you believe on me, a fountain springs up from in *here—*" inside you.

All of you, especially if you live a hot climate, know how refreshing it is to find a fountain when you're thirsty. Geologically, a fountain is the beginning of creeks and streams and rivers. Those all flow out from a fountain. When you believed on Jesus and were saved, like the woman at the well, a fountain was opened up inside of you. Jesus takes this idea even further.

On the last and greatest day of the festival, Jesus stood and said in a loud voice, "Let anyone who is thirsty come to me and drink. Whoever believes in me, as Scripture has said, rivers of living water will flow from within them." By this he meant the Spirit, whom those who believed in him were later to receive. Up to that time, the Spirit had not been given, since Jesus had not yet been glorified. (John 7:37-39)

When Jesus was talking to the woman at the well, He was talking about salvation, a fountain that will satisfy you for the rest of your life. Often, friends that I counsel seem stuck in a constant vicious cycle. They're saved by grace, but they're limping along with no power. They're stopping with the fountain and missing out on the power that comes from the rivers. My desire, with the help of the Holy Spirit, is for all of us to get from the altar into action.

When Jesus stood up to speak on the great day of the feast, He was talking about the same fountain, but He spoke of it bursting into rivers. Not a river—but rivers, plural. Salvation is the fountainhead, but Jesus was saying, "Although you have a fountain now, there's coming a day when that fountain will burst forth into rivers of living water."

"It can't happen yet," Jesus said, "because I haven't yet been crucified or buried. I've not yet been raised. I've not yet gone back to the Father. When all of that takes place, and I am glorified, I will send the Spirit." That's what happened on the Day of Pentecost. Fountains turned into rivers. I'm talking about MORE!

Some of you are satisfied with your fountain, and you say, "Why do I need more? Why would I expect more? Why would I even ask for more?"

Why? Because Jesus said, "I have more—for you. I died and rose again and went back to heaven and sat at the right hand of the Father so you could have more!" It's more than just being satisfied. It's a MORE that allows you to go into a dark world and spread light. It's a MORE that causes you to be fearless and boldly tell someone your story, to be a witness of what Jesus did for you so someone else can be set free! It's a MORE that allows you to walk out into the face of the enemy. Operating without the filling and refilling of the Holy Spirit is like trying to drive your car without gas in it.

Why should you want more? You got it all when you got saved, right? You did get it all; you got Jesus. You received eternal and abundant life. You are on your way to heaven. You got everything you needed to be accepted by God. But even Jesus Himself needed more. He said, "The Spirit must come upon me if I am to be anointed."

- Anointed to preach the gospel to the poor.

- Anointed to open blind eyes.

- Anointed to open deaf ears.

- Anointed to set at liberty those who are bruised.

Jesus knew that even though he was accepted fully, totally, and completely, if He was going to do His Father's work, He had to have the Holy Spirit.

Rivers are mighty things. I grew up in West Virginia, in a valley with lots of flooding. When rivers overflow, they can sweep through a community and take houses, cars, and trees with them. They can move mountains.

Jesus said, "When the Holy Spirit comes upon you, you will receive power to become the kind of witnesses unto me that I've called you to be." It's a power that will give you the perfect balance of boldness and love.

I don't see how parents raise children in these present days without the power of the Holy Spirit. My daughter can't get away with anything. When you have a mama on her knees praying in the Spirit and doing battle in the spirit world, the Holy Ghost will show her things that she needs to know.

I don't see how marriages can survive without husband and wife being filled and refilled daily. My husband and I are passionate, strong-willed people with colorful personalities, which is a nice way of putting it. Through the power of the Holy Spirit, our marriage is as strong and vibrant as we are, but we couldn't do it without Him.

When Jesus was anointed to preach the gospel, the good news, to the poor, to those who had no hope, the outcasts, the vulgar, and the perverted, He never plowed over anyone. He was always kindly and gently walking among them, letting them see His compassion. He had intense compassion for hurting, dying, lost people. When you're operating in the power of the Holy Spirit, you are able to love the unlovable, to love the ones who have accused and abused you.

Too many of us who are believers are walking in less than victory. We're saved, but what about today? What about tomorrow? What about when the evil one comes to tempt us, to torment us, to label us, and to lie to us? How in the world do we battle against that? By our own self-effort?

Unless the Holy Spirit fills and refills me, I am hopeless. A.W. Tozer said, "If the Holy Spirit was withdrawn from the church today, ninety-five percent of what we do would go on and no one would know the difference." How sad. No wonder many churches are weak. How is God going to be glorified if we aren't seeing lives changed?

The Holy Spirit will take our mistakes, our pain, our scars, and turn them into crowns of beauty. My prayer is that we be so filled by His rivers that, as we walk by people, those streams would spill out of us, lives would be changed, and people would be healed.

Many of us are living below our privileges. We live in an age where the gospel is being sanitized, but God sent the Holy Spirit so we can cast out demons, heal the sick, and bind up the brokenhearted. When we have trouble, we don't have to be afraid. The Holy Spirit is our constant companion. We can be fearless. We can make demons tremble!

If the disciples needed the Holy Spirit, we surely need Him now. All of my attempts to overcome fear, anger, and depression in the flesh have never worked. Too often, we rely more on intellect than the supernatural, indescribable power of the Holy Spirit. We beg and plead with God, yet never expect anything to happen. He sent the Holy Spirit so we wouldn't have to limp along and beg.

When you get hungry for God, for more, for the Holy Spirit; when you run out of escapes and get tired of trying to do it on your own, tired of waiting on someone to do it for you; when you cry out and your soul is desperate for Him, for more of Him, I can guarantee you this: God will come down! God will do something unusual! God will take you outside of the ordinary! God will make a supernatural difference in your life!

We honor Jesus when we ask to be filled and refilled with the Holy Spirit. He says he will give us the Promise. It's His gift to us. Wherever you are right now, ask Him. If you can, throw your hands in the air and ask Him for more. Ask Him to fill you or refill you with His Holy Spirit.

Dawn

For forty-five years, God was no stranger to me. I was brought up in a God-loving Lutheran family home, going to church every Sunday and praying every night before I went to bed. I was baptized, went through first communion, catechism, got married, had both of my boys baptized, and I brought them up in church as well. However, it wasn't until February 3, 2017, that I realized how much I was a stranger to God.

My parents will be the first to tell you that my whole life was focused on how I could help others; it was just what I did. At age six, I told my Nana I wanted to be a PT (Physical Therapist). I graduated from Ohio State as a PT, ATC. Throughout my life, I was faced with many trials and tribulations, increasing in magnitude with each episode, which is the foundation of my testimony. I realize now that through all the broken pieces, all the troubled paths, all the tears, pain, and heartache, what I lived through enabled me to help many others. I could truly say, "I know how you feel!" I also realized, this past February, that there was still so much more that I didn't see, that I didn't embrace, that I was also given by God and our precious Lord Jesus Christ. If I had humbled myself to listen, to learn, to understand, I could have not only helped so many more, as one of the Lord's gifted intercessors, but also helped myself.

In March of 2011, I was taken to the ER for emergency surgery, fearing that during a climbing activity when I fell into my equipment, the full body contraction and fear response had caused my Lap Band to slip, which was keeping me from being able to hold down food or water. Once inside, my doctor discovered that nothing was wrong with my Lap Band and that I was in need of a Hiatal Hernia Repair. Upon completing this procedure, he accidentally nicked my aorta, and, of course, my situation became critical. I began bleeding out, and the trauma team was called in, but by the grace of God, my surgeon was able to fix it before they arrived, as time was of the essence. Because the bleeding and situation were under control, it is documented in my medical record that the trauma team decided that their services were not required. My doctor alone completed the procedure. The next part of this story is not documented in my medical record and was told to me by different visitors who came to see me after I awoke. Apparently, shortly after arriving at the ICU, the medical professionals went to turn me to do a post surgical Xray, and blood started pouring out of my chest tube. My aorta had completely ruptured. I was told that it was like a scene from *ER*. People came from all over, I was thrown onto a gurney, and my doctor and the trauma team all came running as well. My doctor opened me up and held my aorta in his hand as they wheeled us back to OR. The trauma team that was still there, as documented by my doctor, refused to assist, saying that only 3% of people survive a ruptured aorta and that I was going to die anyway. I don't know how long my doctor worked on me, but I needed a direct line into my carotid artery to take in 18 units of blood and 12 units of plasma. My entire gut was opened up, and I did die on that table. I was told that I didn't have one single red blood cell of my own left. God pulled me through, and I was placed in an induced coma and returned to the ICU, where I would stay for over a month and then be transitioned to a step down unit.

My testimony contains much more, but this is what you needed to know to understand my life just prior to Feb. 3, 2017. I was told that following the accident, I had only 52% of my lung capacity, and eventually I would have to be placed on oxygen. I lost several years of my memories, I lost bladder control, I was in need of breathing treatments, fast-acting steroid inhalers, air purifiers, and I was unable to exercise or engage in activities without AC for over six years. I couldn't carry on a conversation, let alone present a lecture or walk around the block. I couldn't breathe in closed areas, I became anxious, and it affected my job, my family, and simply my life. I ended up changing jobs almost every year, and with prayer I knew God would protect me. I knew and trusted that when one door closed another door opened. But I just couldn't sleep, I wasn't at peace, and I continually found myself in fear asking why. There were days I felt defeated and just ruined, then I met Jessie, and in September of 2016, she invited me to her Bible Study and First Assembly of God. I was so moved by the choir that even though I can't hold a tune worth a darn, I went to offer my ability to sing a joyful noise. I learned of the Women's Retreat and just knew I had to go. I cleared everything with Darlene and Christy to have my purifiers, my meds, and my breathing machine, and I was told a golf cart would be available if needed for mobility.

I didn't have many girlfriends; I grew up with boys, I didn't relate to women, and I was now headed on a retreat for four days, which I had never done before, and with nothing but WOMEN! I stayed in the villas, so it was less crowded, and planned my arrivals and departures so I could rest intermittently as I walked the grounds. On Friday, February 3, 2017, we headed to the mess hall following our afternoon session, and I had to stop twice to catch my breath during that short distance. Then, once at the mess hall, another break to catch my breath before eating. This was the norm throughout that first twenty-four hours of the retreat. During worship and the song "I'm Amazed," I suddenly took the deepest breathe I had ever taken in my whole life. I could feel the oxygen course through my body from the top of my head to the tips of my toes and fingers. I know in my heart of all hearts, this was the Holy Spirit.

I FREAKED OUT!!!!

I started scribbling in my journal, over and over, "I can breathe!!" I was beside myself; I couldn't stand still, and I lost total concentration. The song ended, and we sat down, and I was on the edge of my seat. My tablemate kept looking at me and finally said, "Are you OK?" I just looked at her and said "I don't know, I don't know, I got to go," so she moved out of the way and said "GO!!" I stood up, left the lecture, and went outside. I was walking, then fast walking, and as I completed that first hundred feet and turned the corner to head up the hill toward the mess hall, I started to jog!!! There was no stopping me, no shortness of breath, no pain, no cough – just simply open lungs. I fell to my knees and said PRAISE YOU JESUS!!!

Of course, I realized I had to get back to the meeting hall. I knew my sisters had to have seen me leave in such a rush and must be worried about me, so I hightailed it back, energy in my step. There to meet me was Darlene. With a huge hug, I shared my divine healing, and together we praised our Lord. I went the rest of the retreat without any problems, and I continue to this date without any problems.

I pray, oh Lord, do I pray and embrace the Holy Spirit. I will not be a stranger to my Lord any more. I have been able to help many more people and in greater, more precious ways in the past seven months than ever before. I see clearly now that it was never my path that I needed to follow, and I can pinpoint the day that Satan got the best of me, and everything about my life was planned; everything I did today was to achieve the plan I set for tomorrow. I understand now that it is not my five-year plan or ten-year plan or even my fifteen-year plan that I am to follow, but rather God's Plan that I need to follow. I pray, I give, and I am learning to fast. I still have trials and tribulations, BUT I have the PEACE that truly does pass all human understanding within me. My LORD, YOU DO AMAZE ME!!

The Deeper You Go, The Greater the Pressure

When you go through deep waters, I will be with you. Isaiah 43:2

But Jonah ran away from the Lord and headed for Tarshish. He went down to Joppa, where he found a ship bound for that port. After paying the fare, he went aboard and sailed for Tarshish to flee from the Lord. Jonah 1:3

Jonah ran away from the Lord. If you're reading this, you probably know that God will go to any length to catch you when you run from Him. Sometimes He will even keep you in the belly of a big fish to save you from yourself. It can take a fish-belly experience to bring us to the end of ourselves and into the arms of the One True God. Jonah, too, finally came to the end of himself.

"In my distress I called to the Lord, and he answered me. From deep in the realm of the dead I called for help, and you listened to my cry. You hurled me into the depths, into the very heart of the seas, and the currents swirled about me; all your waves and breakers swept over me. The engulfing waters threatened me, the deep surrounded me; seaweed was wrapped around my head. To the roots of the mountains I sank down; the earth beneath barred me in forever. But you, Lord my God, brought my life up from the pit." Jonah 2:2-3, 5-6

Jonah ran away from the calling God had on his life, partly because he was afraid of what that calling would look like. We, too,

13

can be afraid of going deeper with God because we fear that it will include deep pain. Few people willingly walk through the fire to be refined.

Jonah also didn't want to put himself "out there." He feared his enemies, and he knew that accepting God's call would place a target on his back. I don't know the thoughts that were running through Jonah's mind, but I can guess:

- I'm too afraid.

- This could hurt.

- I could be killed.

- I don't even like the people God is calling me to save.

- I'm not strong enough.

- I'm not good enough.

- I have a terrible thought life.

- I just don't want to give up my own time to go do this thing.

Where do you suppose thoughts like that come from? You see, not only did God know the plan He had for Jonah's life, so did Satan. For years, probably for Jonah's whole life, the enemy just watched, waited, observed, and studied Jonah to learn his weaknesses. That's what an enemy does in battle; he looks for weak spots and moves in at the exact moment of his opponent's greatest vulnerability.

This is what Satan tried to do to Jesus during his forty days of hunger in the wilderness. Don't you know, if the enemy tried it with Jesus, he's certainly going to try it with us?

When the devil had finished all this tempting, he left him until an opportune time. Luke 4:13

I've learned in my own Christian walk that sometimes it's the Spirit Himself who drives you into the depths of the wilderness, and it was the Spirit who brought Jesus to that place. In the wilderness, Jesus was tested and tried. Satan gave it everything he could to take Jesus down. He tried three different ways to get Jesus off course.

It's important to note that the enemy attacked Jesus when the Lord was at His weakest. He'd been fasting for forty days, and He was weak physically, emotionally, and spiritually. However, we know from what the Bible tells us, that the Devil's attempts didn't work. The temptation ended there. Still, Satan departed for another opportune time.

That completed the testing. The Devil retreated temporarily, lying in wait for another opportunity. Luke 4:13

Satan lies in wait for another opportunity. That's how it works in our lives and in our Christian walk every single day. The Devil is always looking for another test, a better time. He hisses:

- It didn't work today, but I'll tweak it a bit for tomorrow.

- I know more about her now.

- I see her weaknesses.

- I know what makes her tick now.

- I know what pushes her buttons.

- Now I know how to push her over the edge.

- I'll wait for a better time and come back to try what I've learned.

Whenever we taste victory, when we're celebrating that we've made it through this time, he's already looking toward the next opportune time. When there's more talk than prayer, that's an opportune time. When there's griping and complaining, that's an opportune time. When there's gossip and trash talking, that's an opportune time. When there's unforgiveness and a root of bitterness, that's an opportune time. When there's a spirit of offense, that's an opportune time.

Satan's army is creeping in the weeds right now outside wherever you are, just waiting to try and steal the word God has for you right now. Rest assured, God has a word for you today, but just as surely, I know that when you lay your head down on your pillow tonight, the Devil will try to steal it away.

He may says, "That wasn't real," or "Don't forget what you did," or even, "Who do you think you are to receive such a blessing, a princess or something?"

When that happens, you hold your head high and answer right back, "Yes, I am! I'm a daughter of the King, and you need to go back to the pit of Hell from whence you came!" Let's not forget; we already know the end of the story, and we win!

Life can get very murky and confusing, and the enemy loves it. He's the author of confusion, and he thrives on chaos. Do you think Satan and his army are an organized, cooperative group? Do you think they stand at attention and love their master? Absolutely not. They hate him, and they hate each other. There's nothing but chaos and division, competition and bloodthirstiness in the darkness of Hell. Like this domain Satan prefers, our life on earth can also get very confusing and very murky.

The title of this chapter is, "The deeper you go, the greater the pressure." Years ago, I had an opportunity to go scuba diving. I say "opportunity," but I really didn't want to do it. I'm a daredevil who loves adventure. I've jumped out of airplanes and climbed mountains, no big deal, but even with a diving-certified friend alongside me, my massive fear of suffocation held me back. Being underwater for an extended period of time isn't my kind of adventure.

My solution was the bright idea of getting an abbreviated lesson so I could enjoy the thrill of scuba diving. The instructor gave me the basics. He told me what to expect and how it would feel. He told me what I needed to remember if I didn't want to die.

Of course, my heart was about to come out of my chest, and I didn't hear a word he said. He had me put my fins on, which took forever, and he put the heavy scuba tanks on my back. He also put a mask on my face, which for someone who panics when her nose or mouth is covered and has a fear of suffocation, was not a very pleasant experience. He then proceeded to strap me with a lead belt. I don't know how heavy it was, probably twenty to thirty pounds, which is a lot for someone my size.

Before he put the mouthpiece in my mouth, he said, "When you go down, I need you to remember one thing: The deeper you go, the greater the pressure you're going to feel." And then he said, "Whatever you do, don't panic! When I put this in your mouth, I want you to breathe normally." (Yeah, right!) "DON'T PANIC!" And then he pushed me over the side of the boat.

I tumbled and tumbled and tumbled, very rapidly because of the weight I was carrying. I didn't know if I was up or down. I just know that when I got to the bottom, I was in a total panic. I was breathing so fast and so hard that I felt like I was about to pass out. It's amazing that I had enough oxygen left in the tank, because I felt like I'd sucked it all out within the first few minutes.

As I came to myself, looking around, I was surprised to see broken bottles, an old tire, and some rusted machinery on the bottom. I saw things down there that no one at the top could see. When I was up there, in the boat, everything had looked so clear, but when I got down there, it wasn't clear at all. Where was the beauty my friend had assured me I would see?

At this point, I'm panicking. I'm forcing my breathing. I don't know where I am, and I really want to scream. But it's really hard to scream under water.

About the time I thought I was going to lose it or hyperventilate, I felt a hand on my shoulder, and when I turned, it was the instructor. He looked me dead in the eye. I could see his eyes; they were blue, and they were really pretty. But I was really mad.

I was really mad that he had put me in that place. Are you

17

with me? I was angry with him for putting me there. I think if I hadn't been so afraid, I would have hit him, but you can't hit very hard under water. I honestly wanted to kill this man, not to mention my friend who had talked me into this.

So he's looking at me, and I pointed to myself and then upward; I wanted to get out. His face was inches from mine, and he shook his head: No way. Instead, he made a motion with his hands, and I realized he was telling me to breathe. I wasn't going up; that's for sure. Instead, he grabbed me and breathed with me. He helped me to start breathing normally so I wouldn't pass out. That's when I realized that what I was feeling was pressure. It wasn't going to kill me, but I wasn't used to it.

By the way, when you dive into water even a few feet, there's a noticeable change that occurs: The deeper you go under the water, the greater pressure from the weight of the water pressing down upon you. In the very deepest ocean, the pressure is equivalent to the weight of an elephant balanced on a postage stamp or the equivalent of one person trying to support fifty jumbo jets. Now, my instructor had told me it was going to be this way, but I hadn't listened, and he knew I hadn't listened, so he came down there with me.

Once I'd regulated my breathing, I looked at him with a much different expression on my face. I pointed at myself and back up, but this time he smiled and pointed outward. We swam in different directions, through the murky water, away from the broken bottle and the garbage.

Before me unfolded one of the most beautiful sights I've ever seen—the most colorful collection of many different fish, beautiful coral, and underwater plants. I found it difficult to believe that in the middle of the dark, murky depth I'd found myself in, there could be such life and beauty.

After he'd shown me these things, the instructor looked over at me. He pointed up and nodded; it was time to go back to the surface. I tried to push off the bottom, but I couldn't because I was carrying all that weight. Do you know what he did in response? He kept his hand on my shoulder and reached right behind me. He unsnapped the lead belt. He didn't drop it; no, he carried it for me. We both went back to the top. Together.

I never knew all those years ago that I would learn so much about faith in Jesus Christ from one miserable, scary experience. Here's what I learned:

- You had no idea what you got yourself into when you believed on Jesus Christ.

- You just thought it was the right thing to do.

- You wanted to have this great emotional experience with God and just get on with it.

- You had no idea that you have to have the right equipment and that you better know how to use that equipment.

- You didn't know that when you start walking with God, sometimes the pressure can get so great that it can almost feel like abuse.

- Sometimes you think there's no way you can bear it.

- There will be times when you may panic.

- You need to know that <u>you will not go down on your own.</u>

Where can I go from your Spirit? Where can I flee from your presence? If I go up to the heavens, you are there; if I make my bed in the depths, you are there. If I rise on the wings of the dawn, if I settle on the far side of the sea, even there your hand will guide me, your right hand will hold me fast. Psalm 139:7-10

It's easy for us to say that we want to go deeper with Jesus. "Oh, I just want to go deeper, praise God." We say it, but we just stand at the edge. We're toe-dippers, testing out the water one toe at a time instead of just diving in.

That's why, sometimes, He has to push us in, and He knows you didn't listen to him when He told you not to be afraid. He said,

"So do not fear, for I am with you; do not be dismayed, for I am your God. I will strengthen you and help you; I will uphold you with my righteous right hand." Isaiah 41:10 He told you not to panic. He said, "Be anxious for nothing," but He knew you didn't listen to Him.

You may not even be listening to me right now. You may be like my husband, whose mind wanders faster than the speed of light. You may still be down at the bottom of the ocean, imagining the pretty fishies. You might be thinking, "I'd like to go scuba diving one day. I wonder if that would be fun!"

God knows when we don't listen, so sometimes He will push you over the side. Sometimes he makes us face up to our past so we can be fit to face up to our destiny. You may tumble down through murky, dark places. You may find that there's stuff down in the belly of your whale that you didn't know was in there. You'll find garbage down there that nobody else knows about, things you didn't even know about until God got you down there.

You thought that when you said the Sinner's Prayer, it was going to be smooth sailing and everything in you was taken care of. Of course, your eternal salvation and security are taken care of. But He calls you deeper.

But it was to us that God revealed these things by his Spirit. For his Spirit searches out everything and shows us God's deep secrets. 1 Corinthians 2:10

The Holy Spirit who is in you searches out everything and will show you God's deepest secrets. He came not just so you could live a subpar, mediocre, and surface existence. He came not just that you would have life, but that you would live it abundantly, to the fullest. He came that you would grow, and He came that you would be free!

The longer you serve Jesus, the longer you stay down in the depths, the more trash, bottles, old tires, and murky things you'll discover. You may say, I never knew it was like this down here. From up top, it looks fairly clear, but down here, it's a mess. You find hidden things, buried things, avoided things.

Then the pressure comes. The water is murky, and the pressure is too great. You don't know how to use your equipment, and you've never been down here before. You're about to panic, but then—there's a hand on your shoulder, the touch of the Master's hand. You turn around, and He's looking right into your eyes.

You go before me and follow me. You place your hand of blessing on my head. Psalm 139:5

He's not angry that you didn't listen; He already knew. He told you things like, "I have said these things to you, that in me you may have peace. In the world you will have tribulation. You will have trials. But understand this, that in the last days there will come times of difficulty. Be alert at all times."

You may say, "I want out of this. Lord, You've got to get me out of this!" You even speak, "I confess that I'm out of this! I decree and declare that I'm not in this anymore! I'm out of here. Watch this. Look at my faith. I've got great faith! I'm out of this!"

Finally, you say, "No, I'm not out of this. Jesus, please…get me out of this," but He shakes His head and says, "No—not until you relax and realize that I did this before you did it. I know how this is done. I allowed you to come down here so I could show you how to do it."

At some point, in this walk with Jesus, when you're trying to get ahold of yourself, you're wanting to get back to that place where you feel you can worship, you can't. You're too weighed down because of the burdens, but you don't know how to get rid of them. You think, "I can never get back to the surface as long as I have this."

That's when Jesus reaches right around you, and He takes the belt, the lead, the weight; the problems. He doesn't drop them; He doesn't leave them; He carries them. He carries for you the weight that you took down. You see, you can't keep Jesus down. Nothing that you have is heavy enough to weigh Him down.

Here you are, with Him carrying your weight, and you're both floating to the top. You realize, finally, "I know what He meant now: The deeper I go, the greater the pressure. The deeper I go, the more things I discover that aren't like Him." That's not always fun, but I can testify that until you face them, you'll keep going back to those murky waters.

Also, if you don't learn these lessons, Satan will find a more opportune moment to take advantage of you when you're struggling in your faith. Every one of us should expect anything at any time. The devil is always looking for a more opportune moment—to come against you, your family, and your faith. You don't get a victorious, abundant life without prayer, without God's Word, without trusting.

There's one more thing you have to check. Remember, when I got back to the surface after my dive, I was still mad. The instructor had put me through a scary experience. I fear suffocation. I can't handle that; I didn't need that. When I got to the top, I planned to give him a piece of my mind, and I got into the boat ready to let him have it. Instead, he said, "I told you, the deeper you go, the greater the pressure."

Someone reading this is mad at God for what you're going through. You don't think you deserve to have to go through this. You thought you did all the right things. You thought you were faithful. How did you end up here?

Maybe you're kind of ticked off at God. You say you're not. You repeat things like, "Oh, He's good, all the time, all the time, He's good," and, "He's worthy. He's worthy." But you're angry at Him. You don't see the lesson He's teaching you. You don't appreciate that He was there, is there, right with you. It's just a matter of time before He takes your burdens away, just a matter of time.

Here's what I want you to understand:

- The enemy of your soul is <u>always</u> waiting for a more opportune time.

- Sometimes it's the Holy Spirit who drives you into the wilderness, into the deep.

- When you ask God to use you, you better mean it, because He will take you places that can be extremely uncomfortable and painful.

- You are not coming out of it until you trust Him.

- You can't get rid of your own burdens; you have to ask the Burden-Bearer to come and take them from you.

- When you get to the top, when it's over, you are to worship Him, not be angry at Him.

- You are to thank Him—in everything give thanks, for this is the will of God in Christ Jesus for you.

For some of you it's a family conflict. For others of you it's a secret thing. It may be what's happening in your mind. For some of you, it goes way back, maybe even into childhood. For some, you don't know why he left. You don't know why the divorce happened. You don't know why the money is gone. You don't know why the job was lost. You don't know why they found cancer. You don't know why your child or loved one has walked away from God or walked away from you. You don't know why you can't break that habit, that addiction.

There may be a little resentment toward God. I want you to read me loud and clear: He's not even mad at you. I was surprised at how calm my instructor was that day. He could've really gotten wound up with me because I was sure wound up with him. But he didn't.

I want you to understand that God isn't upset with you either. He's not going to smack you around once he takes you out of this. He's going to smile at you and remind you, "I told you that I'd never leave you or forsake you, but you didn't listen. I told you the deeper you went, the greater the pressure would be, but you didn't listen. I told you not to be anxious about this or anything else, and you lost it anyway. But—that's okay. I'm here. I'm God. And you're mine."

Remember, also, that in the deepest and murkiest waters, the instructor showed me something glorious in the depths. In the middle of one of the scariest moments of my existence, when I was carrying extra weight on my back, even right smack dab in the middle of it all, I saw one of the most beautiful treasures of my life. Despite whatever darkness you find yourself walking through right now, don't miss the beauty and hidden treasures God has for you in the middle of what may seem to be one of the darkest seasons of your life.

One of my darkest moments came in 2010. I was the owner of a small business and had just come through the 2008 recession. My product was considered a luxury item, so it was one of the first things people cut out of their budget. My bills were piling up. I began tucking them into a file folder, because after all, if I can't see them, then they don't exist, right? I had several employees and was going into more debt to make payroll. It wasn't unusual for an employee's payroll check to bounce. My property that housed my business had just received an increase in property taxes of a significant amount. There had also been an error on my accountant's end with my payroll taxes, and now I had the IRS calling me. It was a season of hailstorms in our area, and my business property was hit twice by giant tree limbs that did significant roof damage.

Without going into too much detail, my heart was also broken because of limited time with one of my children as the result of a painful divorce. I was also dealing with the very high stress of my elderly parents being "raped" by my nephew who has a drug addiction. He was stealing their checks and their possessions to get money for his habit. They refused to press charges.

My relationship with my parents became very strained as a result of this. I felt frustrated and hopeless. On top of it all, I have chronic migraines. They were happening on an almost daily basis. Migraines can be debilitating. Thankfully, I have medication that helps, but the medication has its own side effects.

With all this happening at once, it became difficult to take my next breath.

I became so consumed by my circumstances that it became very difficult for me to feel or sense the presence of God. I was so blinded by my situation that I couldn't see His hand in anything anymore, and so I came to the brilliant conclusion that God COULD NOT be real. It had been a fairy tale that I had foolishly believed. (Never mind everything that He had done for me my entire life. I couldn't conjure even one of those accounts in my remembrance.)

When I came to this brilliant conclusion, I felt such a dark and cold despair.

It was unlike anything I'd ever experienced. Total void. No hope. No point to anything. Just a meaningless existence. I am ashamed to admit that I actually considered taking my life. I tried to convince two of my best friends that they had also been wrong about God. It was all lies! I know they were worried. They were actually terrified. They didn't even recognize me.

One afternoon, I became so weighted down with the discouragement and the impossibility of everything that I left work and went home to just escape. I went into my bedroom and threw myself onto my bed. (I have a light blue bedspread with blue and white pillows.)

I was mad. I was terrified. I cussed and cried my eyes out. I sobbed until my throat and my eyes were raw. I glanced at my bedside table and saw my Bible out of the corner of my eye. With sarcasm, I reached for it and said, "Oh, this should be good."

Let's see what "You" have to say. Of course, since there is no God, there is no "You." But I opened it anyway. I opened to Isaiah 54. The first verse says: "Oh Sing, barren woman." With much ire, I thought, "You've got that right." I went on to read things like "enlarge the place of your tent" and His "unfailing" love. It spoke of His "compassion,"

As I skimmed the verses, I saw things about being rebuilt with beautiful stones and jewels. There were promises about my children. There was talk of my vindication. "Blah, blah, blah."

I don't care about any jewels or stones. I'm sick of the promises. I need something real! And then my eyes landed on this little line:

"For a brief moment I abandoned you, but with deep compassion I will bring you back. In a surge of anger I hid my face from you for a moment. (Isaiah 54:7-8)

And that was it. That was what I needed.

Now, you would've thought that the promises and the talk of the future and all that would have been what pulled me out of the abyss, but it was God admitting and acknowledging to me the truth of what I felt – His absence.

I now know that He has never left me nor forsaken me, but I also now know that He can get quiet sometimes, and He's shown me that He gets quiet for our good and for His glory. You see, He had some marvelous and beautiful work He needed to do in me, and the only way was to take me deeper into the murkiest of the murky waters. Although I was scared out of my mind and wasn't sure I would survive it, He was with me the whole time.

Watch this: After reading this Scripture and at least coming to grips with the fact that He does exist, I had no emotional high or any solution to my problems. ALL I had at this point was Him. For better or worse, I had Him. And that had to be enough.

I didn't feel anything, really. Just resolve.

I even said to Him, "If you never do another thing for me, if you leave me right here in this place, I will still love you. I will still worship you. As long as I know I'll be with You forever. Fine."

One of the friends that I had tried to convince that God was a hoax talked me into going to a women's retreat the following weekend. I had no money, so someone had to pay my way. I'm not going to lie. I went with an attitude. The last thing I wanted was to be around a bunch of women talking about their problems.

The first night, as the speaker began, it was obvious that she was struggling with what she was going to say. I know this woman. She's an incredible speaker and teacher. Finally, she closed her binder and said this: "I don't know who this is for, but God has turned my attention to Isaiah 54." Ok.

So, yeah, I had a few chill bumps at this point. And then she stopped again and said this: "I don't know who I'm talking to, but God would say to you, 'I have collected every tear that you have cried on those blue and white pillows. I've never left you. I'll never leave you.'" Yeah, so I'm in the floor weeping at this point. I'm told that she went on to say some things about real estate that absolutely had to do with my situation, but I wasn't even in the room anymore. I was at the feet of Jesus.

My circumstances didn't change immediately, but I felt the hand of the Master on my shoulder. He carried my weight, and He showed me beautiful things in the midst of a lot of ugly.

Billy Graham tells a true story he heard from a pastor in Glasgow, Scotland. A woman in this pastor's parish was in financial difficulty and behind on her rent, so he took up a collection for her in his church and went to her home to give her the money. He knocked and knocked, but there was no answer, so finally he went away. The next day, he encountered the woman at the market. "Why, Mrs. Green," he said, "I stopped by your house yesterday, and I was disappointed that there was no answer."

The woman's eyes widened as she said, "Oh, was that you? I thought it was the landlord, and I was afraid to open the door!"

Ray Stedman commented, "The riches of God have been made available to us in Christ, yet most of us shrink back from receiving all God eagerly wishes to place in our hands. The riches of God cannot help us until we open the door of our hearts." That's exactly what I want us to do.

God is calling us to open the door of our hearts. As you think about this chapter, there is going to be a moment that you know will be your moment to come in faith and say to God, "If You go with me, I'll go. I'll let you take this lead weight off me, and I'll let You carry it." This has to be your choice, your sacrifice, and your surrender. It's your moment of truth, your decision to completely open your entire heart to God.

When I jumped in, even in the middle of moments that I thought I wouldn't be able to breathe, moments that I actually tasted fear—in the middle of it all—He showed me a glimpse of my tomorrow. He sought me out. He used others to speak to me, and He showed me Himself. When you reach your moment of surrender, you too will receive a treasure in return. I don't know exactly what it will be, but I know that you can trust the Holy Spirit to give you gifts beyond imagining. Just grab onto everything He has for you. Take hold of Him.

He calls you by name. Maybe you've been called names that aren't from God, labels that others have put on you or that you've put on yourself. If you let Him, God will give you a new label, a new word from your Father.

And I will give you treasures hidden in the darkness—secret riches. I will do this so you may know that I am the Lord, the God of Israel, the one who calls you by name. Isaiah 45:3 (NLT)

I want to ask you a question: Have any of you misjudged the situation that you're in? You thought it was bad, but God calls it good. I've certainly had some very intense questions for God myself. I've been angry and aggravated with Him. I know what that feels like, but He says, "If you're going to follow Me, you've got to trust me, even when you don't see Me."

When you turn to Him, He may or may not take you up to the top. He may or may not make you feel giddy right now. The most important thing to remember is that the only reason you are where you are right now is because God is working stuff out of your life.

I promise you that Jesus is not disturbed in Heaven. He isn't nervous. He's not anxious. He's not upset. No matter what you're facing, no matter what you bring, He isn't wringing His hands trying to think about what He's going to do to bail you out. He is at perfect peace. And He will keep you, who keep your mind on Him, also in perfect peace. Even in the deep.

Sharon

When He Stirs the Waters

Something was happening at this retreat. Something undeniably powerful was beginning to surge in a most unusual, yet gentle, way. The Holy Spirit had begun doing a deep work. The response was interesting, oscillating from full-out abandon to stoic unfamiliarity, yet we all knew it was God and God alone.

Our morning session was coming to an end, and we were scheduled to go to our small groups. As I was standing at the back of the room, I could sense that we needed to change direction. I asked someone to tell Christy what was happening and ask if we could do this. We needed an altar time, and we needed it now. We needed to toss our agenda and allow the Holy Spirit this divine moment. I shared what I was feeling with another team member, who was in complete agreement, sensing the same thing. I took a note to our speaker and it said, "OPEN THE ALTARS." As she did, there was immediate response. Prayer team members went into action.

While this was happening, I walked to the window, and as I looked out on the normally very calm river, it was churning. There were literally waves coming toward where we were. The sun was out, but there was a physical change in how that river looked. At that moment, the Holy Spirit said, "Take them to the river and symbolically step in to it, sealing the work I am doing."

I went to the front and said that exact thing to the ladies. They began to move out and walk down to the river. I got held up a bit so didn't get to go immediately, but when I did, what I saw was incredible. Groups of ladies had joined all over the beach. Some were praying, some were singing, all standing in the river. They had crossed over, and as they stepped in, God was moving!

Prior to this service, my sister, Jodi, had poured out her heart in regard to some things she was struggling with. Jodi is not an overly emotional person, so when she emotes, it's the real deal. I had been praying with her at the altar, and I knew God was doing a deep, deep work in her. As I stood on the shore, I looked over and I saw her take her belt off. I felt the Holy Spirit say, "She's going in." I watched as Jodi began her walk of surrender. I didn't know then how accurate those words were. She walked in to this VERY COLD river and stopped at her knees. (I remember standing there quietly saying, "Keep going. Keep going.") She then walked in to her thighs and stopped, raising her hands. One of our ladies was capturing what was taking place on film, and I went to her and asked her if she would discreetly capture this so Jodi could have it later to remember. The picture still gives me chills. At that moment, Jodi walked out and dove under the water. Understand that this all took quite a while – probably 10-15 minutes.

I began to weep for her, not knowing what had drawn her out there, but sensing that her life was changed forever. The Holy Spirit again prompted me and said, "Go to her." (I had a little discussion with the Holy Spirit because I hadn't brought a lot of key clothing, and going to her meant some things were going to get wet for which there were no replacements…but when the Holy Spirit speaks, you go.) I waded out to her, and she was in the water laughing, crying, rejoicing because in that moment she had surrendered the most precious things in her life to God. The things she had held most tightly, she was giving over to Him. She was realigning her life in the proper order. She was feeling the release and the peace of knowing that control had been relinquished and now belonged to Him. As I held her in that water, I could literally feel the power of God all over her. I honestly can't remember words that we exchanged, but we shared a glorious moment that has cemented our friendship in ways that cannot be explained! The odd thing is, once Jodi got in the river, the river calmed right down with no more waves. Hmmmm.

That night, Jodi picked up her rock. (There were rocks for

everyone to take that had a word and a Scripture on them. The words were face down so you didn't know what word you were getting until you picked it up.) When she turned her rock over, I saw a look of shock on her face. She looked at me and held up the rock. It said "REDEEMED." God's plan, for sure, because that was a weekend of incredible redemption in her life. And it was a word He had spoken to her prior to the retreat. He began a work there that has continued to manifest itself in the most amazing ways. To say that I was privileged to be a part of that is an understatement. Truly God's best is yet to come!

Jodi

I didn't want to go to this retreat; I was sick as a dog and absolutely didn't want to be there. On the car ride up, we began discussing tattoos. I have wanted to get one that says "Redeemed" for a long time.

After the first morning session of the retreat, in our cabin, my roommates and I began discussing marriage and our children. I shared about the betrayal in my own marriage and how God had redeemed it, redeemed my husband, redeemed my husband's life and his soul.

I have three sons and had the privilege of being home with them, but they were my everything and had become my identity. I had a good marriage. We had agreed that when the children were gone, THEN we would take time for us. As the weekend unfolded, the Lord revealed to me how still, even after boys had left home, my husband was still getting leftovers. My sons were still my everything.

At the evening service, the praise and worship was amazing. Afterward, Christy, in her raw way, began to speak. More accurately, she began to speak to me. I said out loud at my table, "Are you kidding me? Stop it!" My friend beside me looks in my face and says, "Boom!"

From Christy's podium was a decorative river flowing into a faux river at the altar. In the river were rocks that she explained had been prayed over. There was a single word on each of them with a scripture reference on the back. Christy encouraged ladies to come pick one up at the Holy Spirit's leading any time throughout the weekend. She made it clear not to turn them over and try to pick the word we wanted. Just bend over and pick one up knowing that it's the one God has for you.

At the end of that evening service, Christy called us to the altar. I began to hear in my spirit, "Come to the altar and lay it down." I heard it again. I heard women weeping and crying out to the Lord, and I found myself getting out of my seat. I didn't know why.

My friend came up beside me, and I said to her, "I can't believe Christy just called me out." I began to feel tingling from the soles of my feet up my legs. I'm diabetic.

As I was worshiping, Sharon began laying hands all over my body, praying for me. I told her I needed to get my glucose tablets. She followed me and said, "This is not over; this is the enemy distracting you." We were both weeping.

Others were still praying. Many had already left. Sharon asked me if I had received the baptism of the Holy Spirit. I told her I had as a child. She asked if I was accessing His power. I told her, "I'm not."

She told me, "That's your problem!" I felt a prodding to go pick up my stone.

"Lord if this you and you have something for me, let me know it's you." I went to the riverbank and closed my eyes. I didn't even know if there was a stone where I was reaching. I bent down and hid it in my hand. I didn't look till I got back to my seat: "Redeemed."

I slammed my hand on the table, "Stop it! Stop it right now!" My friends came running. I showed them. We all began to weep. I couldn't believe it, but I still felt a voice in my spirit telling me, "Lay it down." But I went back to the cabin and placed my rock on my pillow.

At the morning session, what began as a reverent service erupted! Someone at the microphone said they felt that we had to actually go to the river. There is a lake on the property. I couldn't get out of the building fast enough. I ran. I stood at the bank with hands out, palms open, weeping from the gut. I was the first one out in the water. People were worshiping and weeping and praising and praying. I told the lady beside me, "I think I'm supposed to go all the way out there." She told me I better be obedient and to go.

People had begun leaving for lunch by this time, but I heard the wooing. "Come." I took off my hat and belt and my insulin pump. It was if the Lord was crooking His finger and grinning at me: "Come." I went out to the waist: "Come." Up to the thighs: "Come on, Jodi."

I dove in. I felt like I was under forever. I knew that I was being stripped, layer by layer. All the hurt, disappointment, craziness. I came up out of the water. It was the deepest release. "Jesus. Jesus."

My friend Sharon came out to me. "Are you ok? Do you want me to baptize you?" she asked.

I laughed. "Are you kidding? He just did it all!" I began to burst out in uncontrollable laughter.

In the evening service, the worship again was phenomenal. As Christy came to speak, there was such a sweet presence of the Lord. Again I heard the voice: "Come to the altar and lay them down." I stayed back at the altar call. I felt hands on my back, but then the person left. Ten minutes later, they came back.

Christy was behind me and said, "You need to get out of your seat and go lay prostrate before the Lord." I knew in that moment what He was calling me to lay down: Joshua, Jacob, and Zachary – my sons.

"No, Lord." But I stepped out after Christy told me to. I went to the altar and lay flat on my face. He showed me that I had to lay down my idols – my sons.

"Lord, please no. They're mine."

The Lord said, "Ok, Jodi, it's either them or Me. They're not yours anyway. Lay them down."

I spoke their full names, and there was such a release in my soul. The sweetest peace flooded my soul. I could see clearly now. For twenty-eight years, my kids had been my God, and my husband had been getting all the leftovers for all these years.

I called him at 1:00 am. "I'm so sorry. I need to know that you forgive me." He told me I needn't say another word. That night I had the best sleep I'd ever had.

At a place I didn't want to go to start with, God redeemed everything. Things will never be the same.

Do You Want to Be Made Well?

Now it's time to press in a bit more. To get to higher places in our walk with God, we have to go to deeper places with Him. If we truly want to wade beyond the shallow waters, we have to honestly acknowledge where we are. Going deeper means knowing without a doubt that there is nothing we have ever done or could ever do that would cause God to love us any less or more than He does in this moment.

After this there was a feast of the Jews, and Jesus went up to Jerusalem. Now there is in Jerusalem by the Sheep Gate a pool, which is called in Hebrew, Bethesda, having five porches. In these lay a great multitude of sick people, blind, lame, paralyzed, waiting for the moving of the water. For an angel went down at a certain time into the pool and stirred up the water; then whoever stepped in first, after the stirring of the water, was made well of whatever disease he had. Now a certain man was there who had an infirmity thirty-eight years. When Jesus saw him lying there, and knew that he already had been *in that condition* a long time, He said to him, "Do you want to be made well?" The sick man answered Him, "Sir, I have no man to put me into the pool when the water is stirred up; but while I am coming, another steps down before me." Jesus said to him, "Rise, take up your bed and walk." And immediately the man was made well, took up his bed, and walked. John 5:1-9

Are you believing for God to do something supernatural in your life? He already has, but it's not over. We serve a supernatural God, so we should expect supernatural things. I'm not believing for things I can do. I'm not believing for things I can orchestrate. I'm not believing for things I can make happen. I'm believing for God to come and touch my life this very day and to do something that's not natural, but supernatural. Are you?

In this story, we have a crippled man. The Bible says that crippled man had been doing the same thing for thirty-eight years. For all that time, he had just been going to the pool, and he had his little spot where he just sat and waited. He did the same thing, over and over. Year One: No breakthrough. Year Two: Still no breakthrough, no healing. Year three: Still no miracle, no breakthrough. Year Four, Five, all the way through thirty-eight years of believing for something to happen. Thirty-eight years of believing that he's going to get into the water and get healed, that his moment is going to happen, that he's going to encounter the breakthrough. Thirty-eight years of watching everyone else get their breakthrough and their healing.

I believe that to get our breakthrough, to go deeper with the Lord, there are some things we need to take and some things we need to leave. I don't want anyone reading this to miss what the Holy Spirit has for you today. I don't want anyone to do what this man did for thirty-eight years and miss out on one more day of your breakthrough.

The first thing I want to show you in this story is that you have a crippled man by the pool. Jesus goes up to him and asks him a question. By the way, when Jesus asks a question, it's not because He's looking for an answer. Jesus already knows the answer to every question. What Jesus is doing is trying to invoke a level of faith within this man that's so great that he will declare what it is that he's believing for. Today, some of you need to declare, out loud, what it is that you're believing for.

Jesus goes up to the man and asks, "Do you want to be made well?" Naturally, the man responds, but the first thing he says is, "Whenever the water stirs, someone always cuts in front of me." Jesus asks a question, but the man doesn't give Jesus an answer; he gives Jesus an excuse.

If you want to walk away from this book and miss out on your healing, miss out on your miracle, miss out on your breakthrough, just find an excuse. Find a reason why someone else is going to get it, but you're not. Find a reason why that type of blessing doesn't run in your family. Find a doctor who will tell you it's a diagnosis that can't be changed. Find a reason you're not gifted or talented enough. Find a reason that you've not been given the same opportunities that someone else has been given. Tell me:

- It's just a generational thing that runs in your family.

- You're a single parent.

- Your job doesn't pay you enough.

- You grew up on the wrong side of the tracks.

- It's your husband's fault.

- It's your boyfriend's fault.

- It's your mama's fault.

- It's your daddy's fault.

- It's your kid's fault.

If you want to miss what God has for you today, for this year, for your life, just come up with an excuse.

Benjamin Franklin said, "He that's good at making excuses is seldom good at anything else." Excuses are nails to build a house of failure. You have to make a decision to leave your excuses behind. You have to make a decision to leave your reasons why not behind.

When you focus on the excuse, you're allowing the facts to get your attention and not the truth. There's a big difference between fact and truth. Fact is based on the practicality of what is going on in front of you. Truth is based on supernatural power written in the Word of God. The Bible doesn't say, "You will know the facts, and the facts will set you free." The Bible says, "You will know the truth, and it's the truth that will set you free."

You've got to make a decision that you are going to put truth in front of you and that you will let the truth of God's Word light your path. You have to make the choice to walk in the fullness of what God has for you. I'm believing for the supernatural for your life, but those things aren't going to happen if you focus on the excuses. You can't have a victim mindset. Someone with a victim mindset always has a reason why everyone else gets their miracle and they don't.

The man at the pool had a victim mindset. This is the part of the story I just don't get. Jesus had a reputation for healing people. If I were paralyzed, a crippled or sick woman, and Jesus, who is God in the flesh, comes up to me and says, "Do you want to be made well?" I'm thinking, this is my moment! I'm saying yes! Yes, I want to be made well!

Isn't it crazy that this man has the Healer Himself come up to him and ask, "Do you want to be made well?" but this man is so blinded by his excuse that he can't even give Jesus an answer? That's what excuses will do. This is a classic trick of the enemy. Excuses will blind us so all we can see are the reasons why not. If you want to miss your miracle, if you want to miss your healing, if you want to miss your breakthrough—find an excuse.

Another thing we are told in this story is that this man has been coming to this water for thirty-eight years. He has accepted where he is. He has accepted his situation as final, that his challenges, difficulties, and limitations are just the way it is. This is just his cross to bear. If you don't want to miss what God has for you, for your life, then you have to leave this idea that the situation you find yourself in is final. God wants you to know and believe that He has something greater for you. Your journey is not your destination. You may be going through some challenges, but your journey is not where God has called you to end up.

Remember the Master's hand on your shoulder, pointing that it's time to go back up. I believe that for some of you, maybe all of you reading this, that time is now. I want, with the help of the Holy Spirit, to stir up your faith. You serve a God of the supernatural. He's calling you to new territory. Don't accept where you are or that it's always going to be this way.

In Matthew we are given the outline of how we are to pray. Jesus said to the disciples, "Pray 'Your kingdom come, Your will be done, <u>on earth</u>, as it is in heaven.'" So what do you have to believe for? You have to believe for heaven on earth. When you pray, if you understand who you are as an ambassador and daughter or son of the Most High God, what you're doing is standing on earth and reaching up to heaven, and every time you pray, you're pulling something of heaven down to earth for your situation.

Your kingdom come, Your will be done—when you do that over your family, you are declaring heaven over it! Do not accept anything less than heaven. Is there any lack in heaven? Is there any sickness in heaven? Is there any disunity in heaven? Are there any lost people in heaven? Then why would you believe that and accept that for your family? Why would you accept division in your family? If there's no division in heaven, I don't know about you, but I'm not going to accept that over my family. I'm going to declare the Word of God over them: "As for me and my house, we will serve the Lord." That's what the Word says, and you call down heaven over your family. You can call down heaven over your finances, too. What does the Word say? "Pressed down, shaken together, and running over."

Christians will say, "I guess that's just my cross to bear." That's code for, "I'm just going to stay here. This is just what God has for me." You think your Heavenly Father is going to dish out lack to you? If God's Word is true and God tore the veil so that you could not only live, but that you'd live in abundance and fullness, then that's what we have to stand on.

God is not a liar. The thing about the cross is, yes, it was something Jesus bore, but the cross also represents the greatest victory that Jesus walked in. Your cross to bear is not what you're called to walk in for the rest of your life. It might be something that you have to walk through, but there's victory on the other side of it, so that you can walk through a test to get to a testimony.

That very thing can become the greatest victory you've ever known when you decide you're not staying there. "I'm not staying here. My family's not staying here. We're walking through this now, but I refuse to accept it." We've got to get that tenacity in our spirits.

Too many times, we eat what the Devil puts in front of us. We just feed on it. "Yeah, you know what, this is just the way it is." We need to find that spirit inside of us that says, "I'm not taking that. That's not heaven; that's not in my house. That's not heaven; that's not going to be in my life."

Another thing happens in the story when Jesus asks the man, "Do you want to be made well?" The crippled man, in his excuse, says, "Every time I go to get there, there's no <u>man</u> to get me there. There's no <u>man</u> that can get me to the water."

One of the things you need to leave behind is looking for a man for your breakthrough. Are you looking to a pastor to bring about the breakthrough in your life? Are you looking to your spouse, mom, dad, boss, or small group leader? Are you looking to a man for your breakthrough?

I think that sometimes, instead of persevering in our spirit, we wait for a man to come. We wait for that guest preacher to come. We wait to get prayed for by that one person for healing, rather than believing for healing ourselves. We wait until the pastor has just the right altar call, rather than spending our own time pressing in deeper in our secret place, if we even have a secret place.

We need altar times and pastors and small group leaders, but I do believe it's a strategy of the Devil to make us think we have to go through hoops, that we can't get ourselves into the throne room of God. I believe it's the Devil's strategy to make us believe our breakthrough is only going to come from the preacher on the stage.

I want us to understand that we don't have to go through a preacher or a priest or a leader or anyone else to connect right to heaven. We go through Jesus Christ, who is the Son of God, who died on the cross. I can step into a breakthrough myself when I understand what Jesus did for me. God can show up in your car on your ride to work. He can show up in your house if you make a decision that says, "I'm going to have my breakthrough, right here, right now, and I'm not looking to a man or woman to get me to it."

Some of you are waiting on a man of God when you need to get hungry for a move of God. Some of you need to get your spirit so stirred up that you say, "If God uses a church experience, a pastor, a speaker, a teacher, great! But if He doesn't, I'm going to dig in myself, get on my knees myself, before God. I'm going to fast. I'm going to seek the Lord myself." Don't wait for a man.

I get it; there's power in prayer. There's power in someone praying for you, but I want you to understand that the person sitting next to you has the same power inside of them to pray for you as the pastor does. You need to make a decision not to wait.

Back to our story. I like to put myself in these stories. You have a pool there, and you have all these sick people. You have this crippled man. You have blind men. Sick people of all kinds. So, if I was a crippled, and I couldn't get to the pool by myself, I would go and find about three or four really strong, really big, healthy guys. I'm not going to find another cripple. Do you understand me?

This is what I don't understand. He's sitting around the pool, surrounded by people who have the same problem he has. So, when he's looking for someone to help him get where he needs to be, these people can't help him, because they are just as messed up as he is. If it was me, I would be looking for someone who didn't have the same problem that I had. Or, I might even look for someone who used to have the same problem I had but had already made it to the other side of their healing.

You may need to leave some people behind. You may need to find some new friends. When you surround yourself with people who can't see what God has called you to do, pretty soon, you won't be able to see it either. On the other hand, when you get around people who will stir you and encourage you to be what God has called you to be, oh what a blessing that is. Have you ever figured out that those crippled people want you to stay around them so that you will stay crippled, which makes them feel better about themselves? They hate to see you step out of that, because when you do, they are forced to look at themselves. Misery loves company.

Let me put it plainly: If you hang out with idiots, you're going to become an idiot. There's a t-shirt. Keep that in mind. You say, "But I need to hang around them so I can help them. I keep going to those places so I can be a witness, a light. Jesus did it!" Let me tell you something that might blow your mind—you're not Jesus. Jesus did do it, but Jesus was also God-in-flesh. Whatever and whomever Jesus hung around didn't change him; He changed them. If, not if, <u>when</u> you get to the place that you are walking in the same power and the same authority that Jesus did, then, when you walk in those places and get around those people, the blind will see, the lame will walk, the dumb will speak, the deaf will hear, the sick will be healed, and the depression will lift. However, until you're walking in that power, you need to make a decision that says, "I'm only going to hang around people whom I'm influencing, who are not influencing me."

We have to surround ourselves with the right people. That's why we need small groups. Iron sharpens iron. You need people in your life who challenge you, not just people who tell you what you want to hear, but someone who will give you a smack now and then—someone who notices when you've missed church, someone who cares and asks how your walk with God is, someone in your life who's not afraid to get in your face a little bit. You need discipleship. You've got to get the right people around you.

I want people in my life who, if I can't get to the pool, are going to pick me up or drag me there and say, "This is where you need to be." God has great and supernatural things for you. One of the best decisions you can make is to walk this journey that God has you on with the right people, because we all have those moments when we give in to the excuse. We all have those moments when we feel the doubt and the unbelief. We all have those moments when we're feeling down. That's when we need those people to help lift us up. We need someone to speak life, to speak truth into us. Make the decision today that you are going to get the right people around you.

In our story, the Bible says that an angel would come down and stir the waters in the pool. This was a supernatural thing, and whoever got into the water while it was stirring got their miracle, got their healing. This man tells Jesus that the reason he hasn't been made well is that whenever he starts to get over to where the water is, someone cuts in line and gets the miracle that he needs.

Do you ever feel that way? You've been praying for something, for healing, for a breakthrough, for a miracle, and it seems like everyone else is getting theirs? You're single, and your friends are getting married. You're looking at everyone else's families, and their homes seem to be blessed. It's a difficult place to be, but what really gets me about this story is that the man just kept waiting for the water to get stirred. If it were me, in the natural, I wouldn't wait for the moving of the water to happen before I started to move. What I would do is, every day, even if it might be slow, I would make a decision to take one little move, one little scoot. Basically, I would work out, what can I do? I might be believing for this, but until then, I'll do what I can. The man wanted complete healing, but instead of waiting for that moment to be completely healed, I would use what I had to just move me a bit closer, every day.

Now this is the part that we don't like to shout about. We like to shout about the moment that we step into the water and walk out healed and blessed. We don't want to talk about the day-to-day disciplines that we need to practice in our lives, like waking up in the morning and saying, "I'm still believing for this to happen in my family, and it hasn't happened yet, but I'm going to declare the Word of God today. Even though the situation might not be turned around right now, I know that the Word says when it goes out, it will do what it set out to do, and it won't return void. I'm going to send the Word of God out today. I'm going to declare it over my family today." That's what you and I can do today. We can believe our finances are going to turn around—I'm speaking "pressed down, shaken together, and running over" for my finances today, that pool-moving moment. But you know, the Word tells me I need to tithe. We make decisions to do what we can do, what the Word tells us to do, each day. Today.

We do just a little bit each day. We scoot a little bit closer today. When you make a decision to do what you can, each and every day, you get one step closer to your breakthrough. You might not be there right at this moment, but the day will come when you will open your eyes, and you will be in the middle of the moving water. The day will come, and I believe that day is today for some of you, where you are just one step away from the greatest miracle that you've ever experienced.

We love to talk about the moment when we jump into the pool, but we don't want to talk about the small steps that get us there. We want to say, "God, would you elevate me? Would you give me that platform? Would you commission me?" But we don't want to build the character.

You see, your gift will get you there, but your character will keep you there. If you want to walk in the freedom that God has called you to, you've got to have the Word inside of you to walk it out. Don't miss it. Don't just sit back and wait for the water to be stirred. Don't wait for that next church service to happen. Don't wait for the next retreat. Get into the Word. Get into your secret place. Get on your knees. One step. Another step. One more step closer to the breakthrough that God has for you. And it will come. That moment will come, where you will step into the fullness of what God has for you—where your family will be set free, God will touch your finances, healing power will move through your body.

You see, we're all about the destination, but God is about process. The testimony is in the process. The witness is about the process. It's making that decision. God is a promise keeper. We may not get to choose the timing, but that's irrelevant. That's part of the journey.

Think about the Israelites. They could have gotten where they were going in eleven days. If I ask you this question, "Where was Moses bringing the Children of Israel when they left Egypt?" the normal response would be, "the Promised Land," but actually he was headed for Mount Horeb, or Sinai. Remember God's words to Pharaoh, through Moses, "Let my people go, so they may worship me in the desert!" It was not, "Let my people go, so they can inherit a land." Why would Moses take them to their Promised Land before first introducing them to the Promiser? If he had brought them to the Promised Land first, they would have ended up loving the promises more than the Promiser, God Himself.

One more thing you need to leave here today is your weariness. The Bible says, "Don't grow weary in well doing." Here you are again, still praying for that lost child, still praying that your husband will have an encounter with the Lord and become the spiritual leader you need, still praying for your business to take off, still praying to step out of lack and into blessing.

I want to wrap up this section with this: Don't grow weary in well doing. Don't let the enemy get you down. God's ways are not our ways. He operates on a different clock. He's not limited to time. He knows what He's doing, and His timing is perfect. You need to make the decision to believe again and to keep believing. You need to believe that God is doing a work even now. Even right now, God is going before you. Even right now, God is walking before you through the situations in which you find yourself. He's already there. He's been there, and He's making a way where there seems to be no way. God is already in the situation and setting up a breakthrough for you, healing for you, a miracle for you.

You have to decide to get the truth in front of you. Get the truth of God's Word and continue to declare it. It's hard when you're walking through it, but there's something powerful about declaring God's Word. Speak it out every day. It goes out, it does what it set out to do, and it doesn't return void. Even when you don't see it, you need to believe in faith that God is doing it.

God is going to say one of two things to us, "Well done, good and faithful servant," or, "Depart from me, I never knew you." God's desire is to know you. He wants to be close to you more than anything else in this world. God is asking you for total abandonment to Him. Abandonment is forgetting your past, leaving the future in His hands, and devoting the present fully and completely to Him. It's being satisfied with the present moment, no matter what it contains. You can be satisfied because you know that whatever this moment has, it contains God's perfect and eternal plan for you. You are not where you are by accident. God has you exactly where He wants you. Abandonment is casting off all your cares and dropping all your needs.

- "Take no thought for tomorrow, for your heavenly Father knows that you have need of all these things."

- "In all your ways acknowledge Him, and He shall direct your paths."

- "Commit your way to the Lord, trust also in Him, and He shall bring it to pass."

God's call for you today is to go deeper. The deep waters of God's Spirit are calling out to fill the deep places of your heart. Some of you, like Jacob, need to wrestle with God and tell Him that you aren't letting go until He blesses you, and then you need to just worship, like Mary, saying, "Lord, I'm going to break free from my past at your feet." When Mary went home, something was missing on the dresser in her bedroom. She went home with none of the remnants of her past because she had left them with Jesus. The oil in that box was a tangible substance that represented her sin. When she walked in and broke that box, it was breaking free from anything that connected her to who she used to be. And then she turned the memory of it into worship.

One thing we need to leave with Jesus is a Sacrifice of Praise. The very darkest things, our biggest shame, our worst mistakes, are the very things that our Father wants us to pour out on Him. And afterward, that alabaster box will no longer be on our bedroom dresser. What we've poured out at the feet of Jesus stays at the feet of Jesus. He said, "What she has done is a good thing. Wherever the gospel is preached throughout the world, what she has done will be told."

There's a place in our worship where the waves of God's presence can come upon us again and again until we find ourselves in deep waters. Worship is the pathway to deeper waters. With our worship we are creating an atmosphere where God will move us with His presence and pull us in deeper. When you begin to worship, the presence of God will be revealed like rain that will completely refresh you.

Jesus is asking you, "Do you want to be made well?" No more excuses. Surround yourself with people who will help you get to the water. Do what you can, a little bit at a time, every single day. Scoot just a little bit closer every day. What if the man by the pool had just scooted a little bit each day? What if, while he was scooting, the man had offered encouragement to the other crippled people around him to do the same?

Jesus asked the man a question, but He already knew the answer, even though the man couldn't answer it for himself. Jesus said, "Get up! Take up your mat and walk." He's saying to you today: "My darling, enough. Get up! Take up your mat and walk!"

Ellie

This was my first retreat, ever, in my entire life. I didn't know what to expect, so I was expecting everything and nothing at the same time.

On February third, Christy preached and told us to write on a blue card. Now, knowing my background, I'm not that kind of person. I was never taught to believe in these kind of things—writing down your problems on paper, laying them at the altar, burning them in the fire. I grew up in a very religious square box. But that night, God spoke to me and said, "What do you have to lose? Everything you have done this far hasn't worked." So, I wrote down, "Don't want to use my words to damage people, especially my kids. Want to encourage and uplift. Power of my tongue." Christy told us to pick up a rock. Again, not something I would normally do, but then again, I was expecting everything and nothing at the same time. I went up to the altar, I prayed, and I cried. I even had my eye on a particular rock with a verse from Jeremiah. When I closed my eyes and picked up my rock, it said, "Colossians 2:7–Overflowing." Right away, I thought, "It's the wrong rock." However, I immediately felt differently. That night, we were to burn our papers in the fire. Again, not something I have ever, ever done, but what did I have to lose?

On February fourth, Germaine gave her testimony, and Sharon had a vision of us dipping our feet into the river. Before I could even think, my feet were in the water. I was completely out of my comfort zone, but I was there. I kept looking around to check if my cabinmates where with me, when finally, I just let go and said, "Who cares? This is all about me and God! I'm expecting everything!!!" That morning, Sharon was praying for Tiffany Remus, and she looked at me and asked for tissues. I went up, and simultaneously Germaine was anointing people for ministry. When I passed the tissues over, Germaine anointed me. Now, I got annoyed, but she anointed the top of my head, and it was pouring all over my ears and neck. As I got back to my seat, I thought I had just gotten anointed by mistake. I started to question like Gideon. Immediately, Kim O'Grosky came over and asked me if I felt I was being called into ministry. I looked at her and asked, "Why are you asking me that?" She replied, "I don't know, I was led here." I cried, and you would think that would be my answer, but it wasn't.

I asked God that night for a man from up front to confirm what had happened in the morning. Christy's word that night was: Press in Yourself. I was waiting to be called out in public. My entire childhood I had been called out in public. Now I was being told to press in myself.

After the service, I told Germaine about the morning experience. She told me that it wasn't a mistaken anointing. She remembered me; she even said, "It was SO MUCH OIL." She went on to say that she normally doesn't anoint on people's heads. Immediately, God spoke to me about the river rock that said "OVERFLOWING."

By February fifth, you would think I would have had all the confirmation I needed! WRONG. That morning, I started to feel insecure. My cabinmates hadn't waited for me to sit at the table, they didn't save me a seat, and they didn't call me over for a picture. Did they not like me? Christy's message was The Invitation. The process is the most important part of the journey. Have you ever felt rejected, abandoned, like you didn't have a place or people to sit with at this retreat? Sometimes we allow our fear to make us live in exile. "I finally said, "Ok, God, I get it!"

I came home that night full of expectations of telling my husband about all of the wonderful changes that that happened in my life. After all, he had been living with this sharp tongue for fifteen years, and it had done brutal damage. When I told him, NOTHING HAPPENED. He simply said, "Good for you, Honey." Very softly, the Holy Spirit told me, "Show Him." So I started showing him. Little by little.

It's a constant struggle for me to keep that part of my life in check, but Colossians 2:7 has been a part of my daily life. I don't always get it right, but grace is AWESOME! We even have an inside joke within our family now, based on Colossians 4:5, to make the most of every opportunity and always let our conversations be filled with grace and seasoned with salt. When I step out of line with my words, my very gentle, humble, patient, and kind husband will remind me, "a little more grace, a little less salt." Our children will now reply, "That was a bit salty, Mom." That keeps me in check, and I have asked for forgiveness from my children and husband on numerous occasions.

I still don't know what ministry God has for me. It is my job to press in myself until He makes it known. However, since February, He has stretched me like taffy and placed me completely out of my comfort zone. It hasn't been easy, but there has been peace. This retreat was LIFE CHANGING FOR ME!

The Invitation

All my heroes walk with a limp. They limp because their faith was forged in the fires of pain, suffering, and doubt. – C.S. Lewis

Have you ever been to a party or gathering and felt out of place? Maybe you don't really know anyone. You see tables with others sitting around them, having a great time and laughing, but maybe all the seats are full, and there's nowhere for you. You feel like an outsider, and you don't know if you should go sit at the table. Will they ignore you? Will they include you? Will they reject you? Will they think you're not good enough to sit at their table? Have you ever just hung back, like a spectator, feeling like you don't belong?

An Open Table for Mephibosheth

One day David asked, "Is there anyone left of Saul's family? If so, I'd like to show him some kindness in honor of Jonathan."

It happened that a servant from Saul's household named Ziba was there. They called him into David's presence. The king asked him, "Are you Ziba?"

"Yes sir," he replied.

The king asked, "Is there anyone left from the family of Saul to whom I can show some godly kindness?"

Ziba told the king, "Yes, there is Jonathan's son, lame in both feet."

"Where is he?"

"He's living in Lo Debar."

King David didn't lose a minute. He sent and got him from Lo Debar.

When Mephibosheth son of Jonathan (who was the son of Saul), came before David, he bowed deeply, abasing himself, honoring David.

David spoke his name: "Mephibosheth."

Yes sir?"

"Don't be frightened," said David. "I'd like to do something special for you in memory of your father Jonathan. To begin with, I'm returning to you all the properties of your grandfather Saul. Furthermore, from now on you'll take all your meals at my table."

Shuffling and stammering, not looking him in the eye, Mephibosheth said, "Who am I that you pay attention to a stray dog like me?"

David then called in Ziba, Saul's right-hand man, and told him, "Everything that belonged to Saul and his family, I've handed over to your master's grandson. You and your sons and your servants will work his land and bring in the produce, provisions for your master's grandson. Mephibosheth himself, your master's grandson, from now on will take all his meals at my table."

And Mephibosheth ate at David's table, just like one of the

royal family. Mephibosheth lived in Jerusalem, taking all his meals at the king's table. He was lame in both feet. 2 Samuel 9:1-13

Who was Mephibosheth? He was the son of Jonathan and the grandson of Israel's King Saul. He was only five years old when his father and grandfather were killed in battle with the Philistines. In that day, it was customary for the family of a defeated ruler to be killed as well, so that no one of his lineage would be left to reclaim the throne; however, we learn in 2 Samuel 4 that Mephibosheth survived:

Jonathan son of Saul had a son who was lame in both feet. He was five years old when the news about Saul and Jonathan came from Jezreel. His nurse picked him up and fled, but as she hurried to leave, he fell and became crippled, his name was Mephibosheth." (2 Samuel 4:4)

What became of Mephibosheth? He'd grown up and had a son of his own by the time King David asked for his whereabouts. Years earlier, David and Jonathan had been very close friends, like brothers. To honor this relationship and the oath David had sworn to Jonathan, he wanted to find and care for Mephibosheth.

One of Saul's servants was questioned and told King David where Mephibosheth was, so Mephibosheth was summoned to appear before the king. He was petrified because his grandfather had been an enemy of David. He knew that, by custom, he should have already been killed. He came to the king, not knowing what would happen to him or if he would lose his life.

He was a cripple. He had lost his heritage. He lived in a desolate place named Lo Debar, which literally means, "Land of Nothing." Mephibosheth had been reduced to having nothing. He didn't belong, and he felt like a stray.

I can relate to that. On a summer night years ago, two drug-induced teenagers conceived a child in the back of a van. When the girl realized she was pregnant, she tried to pretend that she wasn't until she couldn't. She tried to hide it from her family, but one night her mother opened the door on her as she was bathing. She was discovered. Her dilemma was met with neither understanding nor grace. Until arrangements could be made, if company came over, she was sent to the basement to hide so no one would know her shame. If she needed to be hidden for longer periods of time, she was sent to stay with her older sister. She took matters into her own hands to try to make the baby disappear. She quit eating anything but spoonfuls of sugar. She threw herself down stairs hoping to kill the baby. She climbed on chairs and jumped off, trying to rid herself of the problem. She lived in shame, shame she had put on herself, shame from her family. Finally, the day came that she was taken to a home for unwed mothers. She continued to do anything she could to kill the child up until the day of delivery. She had no memory of the birth or of the sex of the child. Her family told their friends that she'd had a "nervous breakdown." After the birth, when she returned, she had been "healed."

It was a girl. That baby was me. I was placed for adoption and ended up in a Christian home. My new parents were not the loving type. From early on, I understood that something was off. I began looking for love in all the wrong places. I tried being perfect and excelling at everything to get their attention. They never came to any event in which I participated. I spent a lot of time comparing myself to other children and wondering why I wasn't lovable. As I got older, I tried to find the approval I craved in boys and later men.

In my twenties, I met my birthmother. I just knew that, finally, the void would be filled. I knew that she would regret giving me away. I knew that she would remember, when she saw me, that she really loved me. It went as well as a reunion like that can go, but I left dissatisfied. My dream hadn't come true. I still felt empty. I had two families and belonged to neither.

But the King remembered me.

There came a point when I was limping so badly, when I was

thoroughly handicapped, that I felt I could go on no longer. I had tried controlling my chaos with an eating disorder. When I could take it no longer, when I became desperate, the King remembered me. For no reason at all, except that He loves me, He took me in. He told me that I would still have a limp, but that it would be used mightily to rescue more of His children.

Second Samuel 9 describes the meeting of Mephibosheth and King David. This young man humbly bowed, and David told him not to be afraid, saying, "I will surely show you kindness for the sake of your father Jonathan. I will restore to you all the land that belonged to your grandfather Saul, and you will always eat at my table."

Mephibosheth bowed and asked why David would "notice a stray dog like me?" He was promised, by David, that he would be honored with restoration of profits from his grandfather's wealth and would always eat at the king's table. This was despite his low self-worth, his physical handicap, and the shame brought upon him by his grandfather's sins. The king restored everything back to Mephibosheth. My king has restored to overflowing everything that was taken from me, also, in spite of my sins and the sins of my parents.

King David took care of Jonathan's child. Some of you reading need to know that your king has already taken care of the baby you are fretting over. Your king remembers your child, and for the sake of His love for you, He will rescue your babies.

Mephibosheth trembled at the king's invitation. Is he going to destroy me? Is he going to take vengeance? Sometimes we allow fear to make us exiles, outsiders, spectators. We can't believe God would ever want to have us because of our lameness. We get comfortable with our old, crippled lives.

In spite of our lameness, we are invited to the king's table, because of a covenant just like the one sworn between David and Jonathan. God made a covenant with us through Jesus Christ. The gospel takes a man who is so low and lifts him to a place so high! Once we get our crippled feet, our humanity, and our sin under

God's table, we can function as royalty!

It's all covered, every sin—lying, stealing, adultery, abortion; every infirmity—depression, anxiety, eating disorders. There's no place low enough that the table will not cover. It covers all.

Mephibosheth was no longer a stray. Neither am I, and neither are you. There's a place at the table for all of us. No scraps. A full banquet.

Thou preparest a table before me in the presence of mine enemies: thou anointest my head with oil; my cup runneth over. Surely goodness and mercy shall follow me all the days of my life: and I will dwell in the house of the LORD forever. (Psalm 23:5-6)

Put your feet under God's table! Right now, we are being given an engraved invitation to sit at the king's table. But He's also giving us a second invitation.

"If anyone thirsts, let him come to me and drink. Rivers of living water will brim and spill out of the depths of anyone who believes in me this way, just as the Scripture says." (John 7:37-39)

You need to tell someone what God is doing in your life through this book. You are taking the river with you when you close its pages. Rivers of living water are going to spill out of you wherever you go. Rivers are powerful. I grew up near rivers. They can move anything—houses, cars, and mountains.

God has a prophetic word for you. You have been called. Some of you know exactly what you're supposed to do. Some of you are going to start discipleship groups. Others will take up different works, but we are all called to serve in some way. How shameful would it be to bury what God has given us for safekeeping, like the servant in the parable of the talents.

And through the hands of the apostles many signs and wonders were done among the people. And they were all with one accord in Solomon's Porch. Yet none of the rest dared join them, but the people esteemed them highly. And believers were increasingly added to the Lord, multitudes of both men and women, so that they brought the sick out into the streets and laid *them* on beds and couches, that at least the shadow of Peter passing by might fall on some of them. Also a multitude gathered from the surrounding cities to Jerusalem, bringing sick people and those who were tormented by unclean spirits, and they were all healed. (Acts 5:12-16)

Just as David invited Mephibosheth to eat at his table all the rest of his days, God also invites us to come and fellowship at His table. Jesus invites us to come. One day, we will physically sit at our Lord's table when He returns for His bride, and we will share in the Marriage Supper of the Lamb. There is a special intimacy in breaking bread and eating with one another. Christ invites us to share in this special fellowship with Him. None of us deserve a place at the king's table, yet out of His great love and grace, we have a place at His table. You have been given an engraved invitation to sit at the table. No more hanging back, no more trying to fit in. You <u>are in</u>. There's a placard at the table with your name on it.

Mephibosheth put his lame feet under the king's table, and the king's table covered his handicap. This table covers every flaw, every issue, every challenge, every sin. The king brings us cripples to His table. What an amazing honor and privilege our king has granted us! What love is this that invites poor beggars and cripples with nothing to offer to come and dine with the King of Kings? Amazing love. Amazing grace.

Not only does He call us to the table. He sends us out into this dark and dying world. To our families, to our workplaces, to everyone—to invite everyone we know to His table.

Now He who establishes us with you in Christ and has anointed us is God, who also has sealed us and given us the Spirit in our hearts as a guarantee. (2 Corinthians 1:21-22)

In Him you also trusted, after you heard the word of truth, the gospel of your salvation; in whom also, having believed, you were sealed with the Holy Spirit of promise, who is the guarantee of our inheritance until the redemption of the purchased possession, to the praise of His glory. (Ephesians 1:13-14)

Tiffany

I went to the Come to the River Retreat excited and ready to receive from the Lord. I came expecting that God was going to do something amazing, not so much in me as an individual, but in us as a whole corporate group. I personally had been feeling dry in my walk with the Lord and was wanting more from God. I didn't have a clue about what God was going to do in me during this weekend! Isn't that the way it always is?

I need to give a slight backstory in order for this testimony to make sense. When I first got married, my husband was a youth pastor, and I would minister with him all the time at the altars, and I loved it. Often, as I was praying for kids, I would have a vision or impression that God was going to use me in a healing ministry. I never talked about this with anyone and always thought it was foolish and something that I was just making up in my own head. Who was I to think that God would use me in a healing ministry? How arrogant! If I told anybody this, they would think I was crazy and laugh at me, or, worse yet, expect me to pray for healing for them. I knew that I couldn't deliver on that, so clearly this was not from God. As the years passed, God led us out of youth ministry and on to other ventures. We had kids and a business, and life got very busy. I didn't really think about that vision anymore.

About five years ago, during my devotions, God brought back to my remembrance the vision of a healing ministry that He had given me when I was younger. He confirmed that it was given to me by Him and it was not just my own thoughts, but over the last five years, I have struggled with seeing any fruit of that vision and continued to battle doubts about whether God had really spoken to me or if it was my own foolishness and arrogance to think God was going to use me this way. I was continually trying to do everything in my own strength, to do what I felt I needed to do in order for God to use me. I felt like I was hitting a brick wall and couldn't go any further in my relationship with God. By the time I went to the retreat, I was feeling so frustrated. I had basically told God that I was done trying. My devotions and prayer time had become dry and barren, and I walked away most days feeling defeated and discouraged.

The first night of the retreat, Christy asked us what was keeping us from getting closer to God. I told the Lord that first night, "God, I just want to know if this calling is from You or not. I don't care if it is for now or for later; I just want to know if this is a calling from You. I feel like it is getting in the way of my relationship with You. I am doing everything I know how to do to try to draw closer to You, and I just want an answer. If this is not from You, then remove this burden from me, and if it is from You, then confirm it in me. I am willing either way. I just want your will for my life."

The second night of the retreat, God began speaking to me specifically about my doubt and showing me that those doubts were not my thoughts but Satan's thoughts. He showed me that it was the enemy attacking and began to clear my mind. It was like He took away a filter that was causing me to see my thoughts distorted and made me able to see clearly which were my thoughts and which were Satan's lies. He also began speaking to me that I didn't need to fear what God is going to do through me, that God would go before me. That I didn't need to try to do anything in my own power or strength. This in itself was miraculous and would have been enough for me that weekend, but God had so much more in store.

At the retreat, there were stones up at the altar area, with Scripture references and a word on the bottom. Each stone had a different word, and the leadership team had prayed over them and were believing God was going to speak personally to each woman through the stone they received. We were free to take one anytime that weekend. Most people took their rock on Friday, but I waited until Saturday morning. Our cabin was sitting together at a table, and everyone was anxious to share about the rock they had picked and what it meant to them. I went to the front to grab my rock and came back to the table and flipped it over to see what my word was. The word God gave me was "healed." I felt like this was the answer that I had asked God for. I knew I needed to share with the women at my table about the vision God had given me and the journey that I have been on to get answers from the Lord. This was a huge step of faith and obedience for me to verbalize this to these women. As I did, every woman encouraged me and cried and rejoiced with me. It was so neat to see God not only building my faith, but also building their faith at the same time!

The message that morning was given by Germaine Hoffman, who was preaching on faith and healing. I can't remember everything she said that morning; all I can remember is that as she was preaching, it was like God was speaking directly to me. Multiple times, I could feel the Holy Spirit rising up in me, saying, "YES! That's for you!" And my spirit was rising up at the same time saying, "YES! That's for me!"

When the altar call was given, I practically ran to the front and began to pour out my heart to God. I was weeping, saying, "OK. God, OK." (I knew He was answering and telling me this calling was for me.) I was fully broken and poured out at that altar and laid bare before God and His goodness. That he heard me and would answer me! The power of the Holy Spirit was so heavy upon me, I could barely stand. Germaine was praying over the room as a group, but it was like the prayer was just for me. She began to proclaim that God has chosen you, He is going to use you to heal, and it is going to be far bigger than you could ever imagine. I knew this word was mine! I was at the altar answering God, "Ok, God, I won't doubt anymore. I receive it! I receive it!" Sharon McLaughlin came over to lay hands on me and pray for me. As she was praying for me, she began to give me a word also, confirming that God had called me and anointed me, that it was going to be like streams of living water were going to flow forth out of me, and that it was for NOW.

It is so amazing how God does things! He takes care of every detail. Not only did He answer me, but he gave me a whole support system of women at my table that were as excited as I was about what God was doing and birthing in me. They were experiencing it with me! That brought just as much joy to me as His answer did!

That night, Sharon released me to start ministering at the altars, which was such a blessing! It felt like I was home, like it was where I was supposed to be all along. The Holy Spirit was flowing through me during the altar time, and God gave me a confidence and authority that were not my own.

The next morning, Christy preached, and as she was preaching, she was talking about how as believers we are supposed to do even greater signs and miracles than what Jesus did. She gave the example of Peter and how people would line up in the streets just so Peter's shadow would fall on them so that they would be healed. As soon as she spoke that, it was like the Holy Spirit was yelling at me. "That's for you!" And in my Spirit I was jumping up out of my chair and grabbing those words physically out of the air and yelling, "Yes! That's mine!!!"

By the end of the service, the Holy Spirit was on me so strongly that I could hardly hold still. We sang a few songs at the end, and I went to the back of the room and lay prostrate on the floor before the Lord. His hand was on me so heavily that I couldn't even sing. All I could do was to breathe Him in. I felt like I was so full that I couldn't contain what God had given me. At the end of worship, they called for a time of prayer over the leadership team. I knew immediately that what I had been given during worship was for them. I walked up to the front of the room and laid hands on them (so not me!) and basically took charge and began praying in the Spirit over the women (again, so not me). I was praying with such power and authority that I literally was saying to myself as I was praying, "Who is this person?" It was as if the power of God was being called down from heaven, and the only way I can describe it is that it was like the heavens had opened up, the floodgates had broken, and we were practically drowning in the anointing and presence of the Holy Spirit. I really don't know how long we prayed or what happened after that. I just knew that God had taken over. I was moving and praying in an authority that was not my own. I think almost everyone came forward and joined me in laying hands on the team and praying for them. All I know is that God was there, and He confirmed His call and anointing on me, who was struggling with doubt and feeling overwhelmed by the need to DO everything I could to make this calling happen.

63

Since the retreat, God has done so many amazing things in me. I could give a whole list of more testimonies of what He has done. He is growing me in leaps and bounds. I feel like what should take five years is taking two weeks. He is teaching me to be still and let Him do the work. Teaching me to just keep my eyes focused on Him and not the calling, and as I focus on Him, He will do the work that needs to be done in me. Focusing on Him has caused me to be free to just love him. That is all He desires from us—our love, trust, and obedience. He is such a good God. My devotion time has just come alive. It is like God has taken me to another level in Him, and it just makes me hungry to go deeper. I have such a hunger for Gods Word and can't wait to have time alone with him. I long for Him in a way I never have before.

I am learning to rest in Him and not worry about what He wants me to do next, but trust that He will move me and speak to me when He wants to use me. I am learning to just listen for His voice and then obey. God has been whispering to me to be still, and I am enjoying my stillness with Him. It is like God is taking my roots and growing them deep enough for what He has planned for me. I am just happy in Him, and I have total peace about my future. I know that it is not about what I do to prepare, but I am at complete peace knowing that God is doing the preparing, and all I have to do is obey. God is good!

The End is Just the Beginning

There are far, far better things ahead than any we leave behind. – C. S. Lewis

For my thoughts are not your thoughts, neither are your ways my ways, declares the Lord. For as the heavens are higher than the earth, so are my ways higher than your ways and my thoughts than your thoughts. Isaiah 55:8-9

While preparing my messages months prior to the retreat, I felt God pull me away from my studying and research one morning. I've found it best to listen and obey when He does this, so I physically moved to another spot to give Him my full attention. In my spirit, I heard Him ask this: "What happens after?" I knew He meant the retreat.

I answered, "Who knows? But I can't be bothered with that right now. Don't You understand? I have to prepare for this VERY IMPORTANT event!"

He said again: "What happens after?" Ugh. What does happen after? How do we take these women to this special place physically and spiritually and then bring them home to…what? Do they wait until the next retreat? How do we foster the same atmosphere on a regular basis?

I'll be honest; I gave it some thought, but then I put it away. I did say it aloud to my ministry team for accountability's sake, but then I moved on. Not in peace. It constantly nagged at me. You see, I'm a very busy person, and I don't consider myself to be a "women's pastor." The thought of doing something with women on a regular basis was terrifying.

The retreat was incredible, and the move of the Holy Spirit was tangible. People were healed and restored. Ladies were lifted and launched. Gifts were stirred and activated, and relationships began. The attendees spanned the ages of eighteen to ninety-one, and ladies of every color and background participated. I had the constant, humbling thought that I was part of something bigger than me. In fact, by Sunday morning, I literally felt like I had shrunk and Jesus had increased. I couldn't have been more satisfied with the results.

On Sunday morning of the retreat, as the worship team led us into God's presence, I felt a great heaviness, but not in a bad way. It was similar to the feeling a person has before giving birth. I knew that God was getting ready to give me a download. I say that like it happens all the time. It doesn't. This was a very unique moment.

One of the young girls went up to play a flute solo, and I found myself on my knees as she began to minister. The Holy Spirit whispered to me, "I'm completing what I started." You see, when the vision for the retreat began, it had been all about bridging the gap between our women—ages, races, backgrounds, and any other divisive factors. He was showing me that He had done just that.

He also told me, in the way that He tells me things, that the retreat was a small part of it. It was just the vehicle. It was just the hook. He showed me that this was a movement—a movement in His women. As had been prophesied a few years before, it was a groundswell.

I went right back to that moment, months prior, to the morning when He'd asked me, "What happens after this?" Ok. Got it. I knew that my job description had just gotten bigger. Out of *Come to the River*, God birthed River Dwellers, a discipleship class for women of all ages. The response was incredible. We have a revival happening in our women!

Where the river flows, EVERYTHING will live. (Ezekiel 47:9)

This is exactly what is happening. Life is being breathed out and spoken. Women of all backgrounds, both churched and unchurched, are attending. Women from all denominations and of all ages and races are coming to experience what God is doing.

I am humbled by our great God. I am ruined by how much He loves us. I am speechless at how personal He is. I am confounded by the way He takes a message, divides it perfectly and then multiplies it!

At the retreat Sunday morning, while I was on my knees, He also downloaded the entire message of the next retreat.

And then, just because He's a good, good Father, after I had delivered the Word:

We had a faux river at the altar. In the river were rocks that had Scripture references on top that could be seen and a word that was hidden. Each one had been prayed over, and I knew that each lady would get exactly the rock she was supposed to receive. Oh, the testimonies! Well, I didn't take a rock. I was the facilitator, and I was there to serve.

After the altar time on Sunday, one of the women felt led to pray over the ministry team. We gathered in the river at the altar, and she laid hands on us. I ended up on the floor, in a kneeling position. I had just been speaking to the ladies about how Jesus said we would do even greater things than He, and I was talking about this Scripture:

The apostles performed many signs and wonders among the people. And all the believers used to meet together in Solomon's Colonnade. No one else dared join them, even though they were highly regarded by the people. Nevertheless, more and more men and women believed in the Lord and were added to their number. As a result, people brought the sick into the streets and laid them on beds and mats so that at least Peter's shadow might fall on some of them as he passed by. Crowds gathered also from the towns around

Jerusalem, bringing their sick and those tormented by impure spirits, and all of them were healed. Acts 5:12-16

It's important to note that the lady who came to pray for us had been struggling for years with God's call on her life in the area of healing. He had spoken to her and released her in this area during retreat, but I didn't know any of that at the time. While she was praying, I saw the image of these women being so filled with the Holy Spirit that people would be healed just by being in their shadows. I truly felt that her prayers had healed something in me! Just because God is amazing, He was allowing me to be refreshed after a laborious weekend.

In closing, just because God can, and just because He's especially fond of me, right before I stood from my kneeling position, my hand landed on one of the few remaining rocks. There, just for this stray, for this rejected, abandoned little girl, who never felt like she belonged anywhere, who felt like a mistake and was called a mistake, there was a rock for me, and when I turned it over, this is what it said:

"Designed By Him"

Thank you...

To my River Dwellers – thank you for joining me in the "River." Week after week you inspire me to continue pressing on. And special thanks to my ministry team: Sharon McLaughlin – to whom I run for an unlimited supply of words of wisdom; Miggie Castro – the Master of Detail who does the *icky* stuff that I despise; Tiffany Remus – who makes everything beautiful, literally and figuratively; Germaine Hoffman – resident prayer warrior; and last, but certainly not least, Darlene Newcomer – the Queen of Hospitality, but more importantly, it was because of your obedience and your refusal to relent (a nice way to say it), all of this came to pass.